Animal Teams

Beaver Colonies

by Laura Perdew

FOCUS READERS
BEACON

www.focusreaders.com

Focus Readers is distributed by North Star Editions:
sales@northstareditions.com | 888-417-0195

Produced for Focus Readers by Red Line Editorial.

Photographs ©: Shutterstock Images, cover, 1, 4, 6, 8, 10, 12, 14, 16, 19, 20–21, 22, 24, 27, 29

Library of Congress Cataloging-in-Publication Data
Names: Perdew, Laura, author.
Title: Beaver colonies / by Laura Perdew.
Description: Mendota Heights, MN: Focus Readers, [2025] | Series: Animal teams | Includes bibliographical references and index. | Audience: Grades 2-3
Identifiers: LCCN 2023058689 (print) | LCCN 2023058690 (ebook) | ISBN 9798889981893 (hardcover) | ISBN 9798889982456 (paperback) | ISBN 9798889983545 (pdf) | ISBN 9798889983019 (ebook)
Subjects: LCSH: Beavers--Juvenile literature. | Beavers--Behavior--Juvenile literature. | Beavers--Habitations--Juvenile literature.
Classification: LCC QL737.R632 P47 2025 (print) | LCC QL737.R632 (ebook) | DDC 599.37--dc23/eng/20240123
LC record available at https://lccn.loc.gov/2023058689
LC ebook record available at https://lccn.loc.gov/2023058690

Printed in the United States of America
Mankato, MN
082024

About the Author

Laura Perdew is an author coach, presenter, former teacher, and the author of more than 50 fiction and nonfiction books for kids. Her books highlight the wonders of nature and the environment, and call for action to preserve it. She lives in Boulder, Colorado.

Table of Contents

Chapter 1

Crashing Down

A beaver gnaws on the trunk of a tree. The animal uses its strong jaws. Its sharp teeth cut into the wood. The beaver keeps gnawing. The cut gets deeper and deeper. Pieces of wood fly off the trunk.

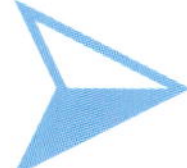

Beavers can cut through a tree trunk in just a few minutes.

Dams usually include wood pieces of many different sizes.

Then the cut is deep enough. The tree tilts. It crashes to the ground.

The beaver keeps working. Its family members work on trees nearby. They chop the wood into small pieces. Then the beavers drag the wood into the water. The wood floats down to where the beavers need it.

The beavers store some of the wood. They will eat the bark later. The rest of the wood is for building. Soon, they will make a **dam** and **lodge**.

Beavers' teeth have iron in them. The iron makes their teeth strong. It also gives their teeth an orange color.

Chapter 2

Family Life

Beavers have strong family bonds. They live together in **colonies**. Most colonies have between six and twelve family members. Each colony includes a pair of **mated** adults.

Female beavers have kits only once per year.

Young beavers often stay with their parents for up to two years.

After mating, the pair stays together for life. The female gives birth in the spring. Her litter often has three or four **kits**.

At first, baby beavers can't take care of themselves. To survive, they need help from their families. Colonies have young beavers born the year before. Those yearlings help take care of the babies. They collect food. They also help build dams and lodges.

Young beavers in a colony play together, too. They learn how to move their bodies well. Young beavers also learn from watching their parents. They learn more about how to build dams and lodges.

Young beavers often swim with their mothers to stay safe.

Most beavers live in ponds. But in winter, many ponds freeze over. So, beavers stay inside lodges. A lodge might be cramped. But life is mostly peaceful. The family has a **hierarchy**. Adult beavers watch over yearlings. Yearlings watch over kits. Everyone works together.

Beavers stay together for safety, too. They can avoid danger. And they can defend their area from other beavers. They mark their area with a scent. That warns others to stay out. If an outsider comes, the beavers may attack.

A beaver can slap its tail on water. That warns family members of danger.

Chapter 3

Building Together

Beavers cannot move very fast on land. But they are great swimmers. In the water, they can move quickly and avoid **predators**. That's why beavers build their lodges in the water.

Beavers can swim up to 6 miles per hour (10 km/h).

Beavers can build a whole dam in less than 24 hours.

Before a colony can build a lodge, it must build a dam. The colony uses branches and logs. Beavers weave the branches together. They pack logs into place. Beavers also use mud, plants, and rocks. These objects make the dam stronger and waterproof.

When a dam is complete, it slows down the water in a stream or river. Water collects behind the dam. That creates a pond. Beavers can swim safely there. The area becomes a good spot for a home.

Next, the whole family works together to build the lodge. The beavers use the same materials that they used for the dam. They use similar methods, too.

Most beaver colonies make dome-shaped lodges. All lodges need thick, strong walls. A beaver lodge also needs an open **chamber**. It goes on the inside, above the water level. The family lives there.

In winter, beaver lodges are warm. Predators cannot get inside.

Some beavers build lodges on the sides of rivers or ponds. Those lodges are not dome-shaped.

Beavers usually stay hidden in their lodges all winter long.

But beavers can enter through tunnels underwater. Their teamwork in making the structure keeps them safe. The beaver family can stay comfortable.

THAT'S AMAZING!

Habitat Help

The beavers' teamwork helps the colony. But it also helps the areas around them. After beavers build dams, ponds form. That creates a new **habitat**. More plants grow in the ponds. And many other animals come to live there. The ponds help during dry times, too. Below each pond, water moves more slowly. There is less **erosion**. That helps prevent flooding.

In these ways, beavers are helpful for nature. Plants and animals depend on them. Without beavers, some habitats might not exist.

Some beaver dams get washed away. Others stay in place for several years.

Chapter 4

Collecting Food

Beavers are herbivores. They eat the roots, branches, bark, and leaves of trees. Beavers get energy from the sugary part under the bark. Beavers eat plants that grow in the water, too.

Beavers' stomachs help break down parts of the branches they eat.

Sometimes beavers dig tunnels in damp ground.

When kits are born, their mothers nurse them. After a few months, the whole colony helps feed them. For example, older beavers collect food. They bring leafy branches and other plants to kits.

Beaver colonies also prepare food for later. In cold areas, their ponds freeze. The ponds could be frozen for months. As a result, beavers can't move through the ice to reach the shore. But they can use the lodge's tunnels. In this way, they can swim into the pond.

Beavers also use the pond as a refrigerator. They take branches down to the bottom of the pond.

Then they tuck the branches into mud. The cold water keeps the branches fresh. The colony can eat the food later.

Collecting enough food for winter is a lot of work. So, during fall, the whole colony is very busy. They work to cut down trees. The beavers

Beavers also dig passages. When water fills the passages, beavers can swim closer to trees. Then they can collect more food and wood.

Beavers' fur grows longer in winter. The fur is waterproof and helps keep them warm.

separate the branches. And they stock up the pond refrigerator. By working together, the colony has enough food to survive.

FOCUS ON

Beaver Colonies

Write your answers on a separate piece of paper.

1. Write a letter to a friend describing the different members of a beaver family.
2. What beaver behavior is most interesting to you? Why?
3. How do beavers get food during winter when ponds are frozen?
   - A. They eat food they stored at the bottom of the pond.
   - B. They catch fish swimming in the pond.
   - C. They break the ice to search for food on land.
4. Why can't predators get into beavers' lodges?
   - A. Predators get tired on the way inside.
   - B. Predators can't find the entrances.
   - C. Predators are afraid to swim in ponds.

5. What does **gnaws** mean in this book?

A beaver ***gnaws*** *on the trunk of a tree. The animal uses its strong jaws. Its sharp teeth cut into the wood.*

A. makes noise
B. sleeps
C. chews

6. What does **herbivores** mean in this book?

Beavers are ***herbivores****. They eat the roots, branches, bark, and leaves of trees.*

A. animals that eat only meat
B. animals that eat only plants
C. animals that do not eat

Answer key on page 32.

Glossary

chamber
A space used as a room.

colonies
Groups of animals that live together.

dam
A structure that stops water from flowing.

erosion
The act of wearing away a surface.

habitat
The type of place where plants or animals normally grow or live.

hierarchy
A system where members of a group are ranked.

kits
Baby beavers.

lodge
A beaver's home.

mated
Paired up in order to have babies.

predators
Animals that hunt other animals for food.

To Learn More

BOOKS

Borgert-Spaniol, Megan. *Beavers: Wetland Architects*. Minneapolis: Abdo Publishing, 2020.

McCarthy, Cecelia Pinto. *Freshwater Biomes*. Minneapolis: Abdo Publishing, 2024.

Schwartz, Heather E. *Meet a Baby Beaver.* Minneapolis: Lerner Publications, 2024.

NOTE TO EDUCATORS

Visit **www.focusreaders.com** to find lesson plans, activities, links, and other resources related to this title.

Index

Answer Key: 1. Answers will vary; **2.** Answers will vary; **3.** A; **4.** B; **5.** C; **6.** B